Identification & Price Guide to
Winnie the Pooh Collectibles

by Carol J. Smith

Published by **Hobby House Press** Hobby House Press, Inc.
Grantsville, Maryland 21536

Cover: Pocket Pooh, 5in (13cm) fully jointed, mohair, limited edition by R. John Wright. All of Pooh's friends will appear in this diminutive size. *Photograph courtesy of R. John Wright.*

Title Page: R. John Wright, circa 1987 to 1989. Pooh with honey pot, tan mohair, jointed with felt bee in ear, white cotton bib, and ceramic honey pot. Mint in box Pooh: $400-500. (*See page 33 for further details.*)

Back Cover: (Top) Unknown maker, circa 1940s. Straw-filled, honey colored mohair Pooh, 8in (20cm), wearing red felt shirt. Very good condition: $180-230. Two-part bank held together with ribbon. Circa late 1920s-1930s. Near mint: $125-150. (Bottom) Gund, circa 1964 to 1968. Woodchip-filled Pooh characters surrounding vinyl carrying cases that came with some of the sets. Very good condition: $15-25 each. Vinyl cases, dated 1964: $20-30. (*See page 9 for further details.*)

Identification & Price Guide to Winnie the Pooh Collectibles featuring Winnie the Pooh items is an independent study by the author, Carol J. Smith, and published by Hobby House Press, Inc. The research and publication of this book were not sponsored in any way by the manufacturer of the items featured in this study. Photographs of the collectibles were from the collection belonging to Carol J. Smith at the time the photograph was taken unless otherwise credited with the caption.

The values given within this book are intended as value guides rather than arbitrarily set prices. The values quoted are as accurate as possible but in the case of errors, typographical, clerical or otherwise, the author and publisher assume no liability or responsibility for any loss incurred by uses of this book.

Additional copies of this book may be purchased at $12.95
from
HOBBY HOUSE PRESS, INC.
1 Corporate Drive
Grantsville, Maryland 21536
1-800-554-1447
(please add $4.75 per copy for postage.)
or from your favorite bookstore or dealer.

Printed in the United States of America

ISBN: 0-87588-417-2

Table of Contents

Introduction

The intention of this book is to provide accurate information on the origins and dates of a variety of authorized Winnie the Pooh and friends collectibles. In addition, a value range is listed for each item that reflects the author's experience in this market. There is a vast number of Pooh collectibles available, but only a few of these items are listed in current books of collectible bears and Disneyana. It is hoped that this book will help fill the existing void regarding one of the most popular bear characters in history.

There is no question that items can be found for less or more than the values listed, but the ranges in this book are the prices most commonly found for these items in the listed conditions. Values for items depend upon several factors. The first factor to consider is the popularity or demand for that item. Plush, ceramics, watches, and artwork are currently in high demand among Pooh collectors. Also collectors who are not limited to only Pooh bear collecting, may desire certain types of Pooh collectibles, such as character watches, or a certain type of ceramic. Another consideration is the rarity of the item. Older (pre-Disney) items were simply not produced in the great quantities of items today, plus many older pieces were discarded or broken, increasing the rarity. However, even more recent items display rarity such as the limited edition R. John Wright dolls.

Condition is another important factor in determining value. Some collectors will not purchase a desired item unless the condition is near mint or better. Values for the pristine conditions should be higher. Not to be over-looked is the sentimentality and love that a collector may have for a particular item or type of item. This desire can surpass all others when a collector is deciding whether the price is worth the possession of the collectible.

The collector can find a wide range of prices for Pooh collectibles, depending upon where they shop. The least expensive sources are thrift stores and garage sales, where the collectible value of an item is often overlooked or unimportant to the seller. Other collectors can be valuable sources of items, but they will want and deserve a fair price for their collectibles. Antique stores and shows can also yield Pooh collectibles at a reasonable price. The higher prices can be found at collectible toy shows, stores, and auctions. However, some items are so difficult to find that your only chance of obtaining them may be through a toy dealer, in which case, the price can be well worth it.

A beginning collector may want to keep costs down by deciding in advance how to limit their collection. They may want to collect only Pooh items and not his friends, or they may want to specialize in only plush (a formidable task in itself). Keep in mind that it is easier and usually less-expensive to buy new and currently available Pooh items. Once they are discontinued, it can be difficult and more expensive to obtain the item due to Pooh's popularity. New items can be found at Disney Stores and through Disney catalogs as well as at Disney Parks. Currently a wider variety of items is available at the Disney Stores more than anywhere else. Sears has been a major source of Pooh items, but the supply is dwindling as the Disney Stores grow. Also some dealers specialize in providing current Pooh collectibles at a discount of 20 to 30% off retail price. The best way to find these dealers is through other collectors or by joining one of the larger Disneyana fan clubs. These clubs publish bimonthly newsletters containing classified advertisements of items for sale. Many dealers advertise here.

The most important informational sources used in this book were old Sears toy and Christmas catalogs, which are collectibles themselves. Sears has been a major retailer of Pooh items in the last 25 years, and many toys can be accurately dated by utilizing these catalogs. Also used were magazine articles, advertisements, and of course, the experience of collectors. However, sometimes informational sources can be incorrect, or just nonexistent, especially for the oldest of items.

One important thing I have learned in collecting Pooh items, is that there is a never-ending supply. There is no possible way to list all the Pooh collectibles in one book, or even in a series of books. It was difficult to narrow the items portrayed in this book to a reasonable amount. Primary consideration was given to more popular items such as plush and ceramics. Also, a separate chapter on **Christmas with Pooh** was created to display the fun collectibles developed annually for this holiday in often limited amounts. A future edition of Pooh collectibles is planned to highlight other subjects such as toys, games, pin-back buttons, jewelry, and posters.

Of course, the major purpose of this book is to provide enjoyment for those of us who love Winnie the Pooh and to help collectors recognize items by sight when they are shopping. The information of the dates and values should be helpful when dealing with items, as a few dealers can be over-zealous in their dating. I will never forget one dealer who insisted that her Pooh bear was from the 1920s, even though he was made by Gund for Sears and stuffed with polystyrene beads (not to mention the fact that Pooh was not created until 1926). An accurate date is vitally important for the collector to decide if the price is reasonable. The next section provides a brief history and date guideline to use as an aid in dating Pooh collectibles. It is hoped that you will have as much fun reading this book as I have had writing it, and that this will help you find, date or value Pooh items, whether you are a dealer or a collector.

A Brief History of Pooh

Winnie the Pooh became available to the world in 1926, when A. A. Milne published *Winnie-the-Pooh*. In the United States and Canada, Stephen Slesinger obtained the rights for merchandising Pooh items from 1929 through 1963. Some wonderful collectibles were produced during this time, including dolls by Agnes Brush, stationery sets, dishes and Knickerbocker plush toys.

In the early 1960s, Walt Disney Productions purchased the merchandising rights for Winnie the Pooh so that by 1964, Pooh items were now marked with the Walt Disney Productions copyright. Featurettes thus far produced include: "Winnie the Pooh and the Honey Tree" (1966), "Winnie the Pooh and the Blustery Day" (1968), "Winnie the Pooh and Tigger Too" (1974), and "Winnie the Pooh and a Day for Eeyore" (1983). In addition, a short educational film entitled "Winnie the Pooh Discovers the Seasons" was released in 1981. "The New Adventures of Winnie the Pooh" has been a weekly television cartoon since 1988, followed by the release of "Winnie the Pooh and Christmas Too" in December, 1991.

The appearance of the various characters has changed significantly throughout the years. The classic illustrations by E. H. Shepard are fondly remembered as a distinct part of many adults' childhoods. Although the stories were modeled after Milne's son and his toys, E. H. Shepard drew Christopher Robin and Pooh after his own son, Graham, and Graham's teddy bear, Growler. This is the reason for the yellow colored Pooh in the illustrations, while the actual origi-nal stuffed Pooh is brown. However, Shepard did model Tigger, Eeyore, Piglet, Kanga and Roo after the actual toys belonging to Christopher Robin. Rabbit and Owl were modeled from real animals, not toys. In the classic illustrations, Pooh may or may not be wearing a red shirt, while Piglet wears a green coat, black shoes, and has a pointed, upturned nose. Christopher Robin possesses clothing appropriate for the times.

When Walt Disney Productions purchased the rights, animators changed the appearance of Christopher Robin to that of an American Boy in the 1960s. Pooh was almost always drawn wearing a red shirt, Piglet was most often wearing dark pink clothing. Early Disney drawings of Piglet also depicted him with a pointed nose, and Tigger as a yellow and black tiger with a normal-sized muzzle and mouth. However later, Piglet's nose became more pig-like and Tigger changed drastically. Tigger's color changed to orange and black with a white belly. His muzzle was enlarged so that he became more expressionate.

By utilizing this information, you can more easily assign a general date to Pooh collectibles that may not be displayed in this book. First consider the copyright markings. I have one bank that is marked A. A. Milne. That, coupled with the information from an independent antique dealer that banks from the late 1920s to 1930s were made out of that material and in that style, allows one to suppose it was made in the late 1920s before rights were obtained by Stephen Slesinger in 1929. Items marked Stephen Slesinger fall within the dates of 1929 to 1963, giving you a gross approximation without further research. When you find items marked as such, my advice would be to buy them if you can. The pre-Disney Pooh items were not manufactured in large quantities and are in high demand. The Disney copyright is found on Pooh items from 1964 to the present. For the Disney items, pay particular interest to Piglet and Tigger. If they appear as described above in early Disney Pooh style, you probably have a collectible from the 1960s. Keep in mind that recently, new items have appeared utilizing the classic style by E. H. Shepard.

You can also learn to recognize a style from a particular manufacturer, such as the plush by Gund, or the ceramics by Enesco. As each chapter in this book is in chronological order, you can follow the changes in the style of the characters as they pass from Slesinger to Disney, and from one manufacturer to another.

Plush Pooh and Friends —
Early Pooh Characters

Plush Pooh characters made prior to the Disney acquisition of Pooh were not manufactured in great quantity. This adds to the rarity of each item, and therefore to its value.

Agnes Brush, circa 1940 to 1950s. Tan felt covered Pooh wearing red cotton shirt with PB (Pooh Bear) initials, wooden, beaded eyes. 12in (31cm). Very good condition: $200-300. Cotton cloth covered Piglet by

Agnes Brush, wooden eyes, 10in (25cm). Very good condition: $200-300. Agnes Brush also made the other Pooh characters as well.

Unknown maker, circa 1940s. Straw-filled, honey colored mohair Pooh, 8in (20cm), wearing red felt shirt. Very good condition: $180-230. Two-part bank held together with ribbon. Circa late 1920s-1930s. Near mint: $125-150.

Gund, circa 1964 to 1968. Woodchip-filled Pooh characters surrounding vinyl carrying cases that came with some of the sets. Top row, left to right: purple heffalump (similar to elephant); brown and pink Kanga with felt baby Roo; orange Woozle (similar to weasel); purple heffalump using trunk as a horn. Bottom row, left to right: pink and black Piglet; yellow and black Tigger; tan and white Rabbit with ears held upright; gold and red sitting Pooh; tan and white Rabbit with ears sewn back; gray Eeyore; gold and red standing Pooh; yellow, white and black Tigger. Some versions are covered with corduroy, some with velour. 5in (13cm) to 6in (15cm). Not shown is a yellow heffalump, a red heffalump, and a blue and yellow snake charmer Woozle. Very good condition: $15-25 each. Vinyl cases, dated 1964: $20-30.

9

Knickerbocker, circa 1963. Gold, 13in (33cm) plush Pooh wearing a blue cotton shirt with a white pom-pom button, black plastic eyes and black pom-pom nose. Tag is sewn into shirt and reads the same as described below. Beige plush 11in (28cm) Piglet with a sewn-in white and red striped shirt, black cotton feet, and black plastic eyes. Marked "Winnie-the-Pooh, 1963, Stephen Slesinger, Inc. Knickerbocker Joy of a Toy." Not shown, but also produced by Knickerbocker, are Kanga with Roo in pouch, Tigger, Rabbit, Eeyore, and Owl. Very good condition: $75-150.

With the release of "Winnie the Pooh and the Honey Tree" in 1966, came a flood of Pooh collectibles available at Sears and Disneyland. Gund was a major manufacturer of plush Pooh in the 1960s, and many of their products were sold through Sears.

Gund, circa 1964 to 1967. Complete set of one version of large Gund Pooh characters. Left to right: 12in (31cm) brown and yellow Owl with vinyl beak, paper eyes; 12in (31cm) brown and white Rabbit with paper eyes; 11in (28cm) pink Piglet with blue and white sewn-in shirt and plastic eyes; 18in (46cm) brown and tan Kanga with baby Roo in pouch; 11in (28cm) long gray Eeyore with cloth and plastic eyes, button on tail; 18in (46cm) Christopher Robin with navy shorts and orange shirt, name written on shirt; 11in (28cm) gold Pooh with red cotton shirt, name embroidered on shirt. Foreground: 15in (38cm) long gold and black stripped Tigger, black plastic eyes, squeaker in belly. All are tagged "Winnie the Pooh, Gund MFG. CO., J. Swedlin Inc." Also available but not shown was a 17in (43cm) tan Rabbit with white belly and muzzle and black plastic eyes. Excellent condition: Pooh, Piglet, Eeyore: $35-45. Kanga/Roo, Rabbit, Owl, Tigger: $50-75. Christopher Robin: $75-125.

Gund, circa 1964 to 1968. Different versions of Winnie the Pooh in the mid-1960s. All are tagged "Winnie the Pooh, Gund MFG. CO., J. Swedlin Inc.," except the second from the left which is tagged "Winnie the Pooh, Walt Disney Prod., Made in Japan." From left to right: 14in (36cm) gold plush Pooh with black plastic nose and eyes; 10in (25cm) gold plush Pooh with fabric nose and plastic eyes; 15in (38cm) polyester Pooh with velcro on front paws, pompom nose, plastic eyes; 14in (36cm) gold plush Pooh with squeaker in belly; 14in (36cm) tan-gold plush Pooh with reinforced legs for standing, pom-pom nose, plastic eyes. Very good condition: $15-35.

Gund, circa 1964 to 1966. Three different sizes of gold plush Poohs, 10in (25cm), 12in (31cm), 22in (56cm) (two styles of 22in [56cm] are shown). The 12in (31cm) and 22in (56cm) Poohs came with either a red shirt or yellow shirt with red and white trim. In foreground are two additional varieties of Eeyores. To left is gray and white 13in (33cm) Eeyore, to right is gray and blue 13in (33cm) Eeyore with original lavender ribbon and name banner on tail. Also available, but not shown, were a 39in (99cm) Pooh of the same style and a 12in (31cm) Pooh with felt eyelashes sewn down to depict a sleeping bear. Very good condition Pooh or Eeyore: $20-40. Very good condition 39in (99cm) Pooh: $175-225.

Gund, circa 1964 to 1966. 8in (20cm) vinyl headed Pooh and Kanga plush roly-polys. Musical bells inside. Kanga is brown and tan with a yellow and blue name-inscribed bib. Pooh is gold with a red shirt with "Pooh" in yellow letters. Both have white felt hands and circular felt feet. Near mint condition: $45-55.

Gund, circa 1964 to 1968. More varieties of Gund mid-1960s Pooh characters. Back row, left to right: 11in (28cm) gold plush Pooh with red shirt; 12in (31cm) yellow plush musical Pooh with red and white bib, 10in (25cm) tan plush Pooh with yellow and red shirt and red stocking hat, bottom paws possess "paw prints," glass two-toned eyes; 12in (31cm) gold fuzzy plush Pooh with red bib; 11in (28cm) gold plush Pooh with red shirt and bell in ear. Foreground, left to right: 9in (23cm) solid gray Eeyore with plastic eyes; 9in (23cm) orange, black and white Tigger, plastic eyes, rust pom-pom nose; 9in (23cm) orange and black Tigger with original name banner, plastic eyes, brown pom-pom nose. Excellent condition gold plush Poohs: $15-35. Excellent condition tan plush Pooh: $85-150. Excellent condition Eeyore: $45-65. Excellent condition Tigger: $30-50.

14in (36cm) reclining Gund Tigger with enlarged mouth and plastic eyes, and a 16in (41cm) reclining Tigger with plastic eyes, brown pom-pom nose filled with black whiskers and a paper mouth. Excellent condition Tiggers: $45-65.

Horsman, circa 1960s. Left to right: Piglet and Eeyore made by Gund, sold at Sears. Piglet is 7in (18cm), pink with a red and white shirt. Eeyore is 5in (13cm) sitting, gray and white with cloth features. Near mint condition: $20-30. Two types of Christopher Robin dolls by Horsman with origi-nal clothing. 11in (28cm) doll wears a yellow and white shirt and navy shorts and came with 4in (10cm) vinyl Pooh. The 8in (20cm) version is much less common and is wearing a yellow and white shirt, purple tie, black shorts. Excellent condition: $40-65.

Gund, circa late 1960s. 8in (20cm) sitting and 10in (25cm) standing Pooh, yellow plush with red shirt, and plastic nose and eyes. Good condition: $20-30.

Left: Gund, circa 1964 to 1966. Tigger and Pooh handpuppets, plastic eyes, pom-pom noses. Excellent condition: $35-55. Peek-A-Pooh changeable doll by Aurora Productions Corp. 1976. Four different views of Pooh can be seen by lifting each flap of cloth. Near mint: $35-45.

15

California Stuffed Toys, circa 1968-1980. 13in (33cm) Tigger in sitting position. Excellent condition: $20-40.

California Stuffed Toys, circa 1968 to 1980. Background, left to right: 24in (61cm) gold plush Pooh with red shirt, (other sizes available in this style include a 15in [38cm] and 33in [84cm] Pooh); 21in (53cm) orange, black and white Tigger standing on hind legs; 10in (25cm) and 7in (18cm) gold plush Pooh wearing red bibs. The 7in (18cm) version is "beanbag" stuffed. Foreground, left to right: 13in (33cm) reclining gray and white Eeyore with black felt mane, tail, mouth and eyes; 10in (25cm) musical gold plush Pooh wearing red bib; 16in (41cm) long standing gray and white Eeyore with black mane, tail and trim. Excellent condition giant 33in (84cm) Pooh: $55-75. Excellent condition other sized Poohs: $10-35. Excellent condition Eeyores, Tigger: $20-40.

McCall's Patterns, circa late 1960s. Left to right. In addition to Pooh in the same packet, were patterns for Kanga, Baby Roo, Piglet, Tigger, and Eeyore. The Eeyore on the right follows the McCall's pattern but is tagged "Whippersnappers." Excellent condition: $15-25.

Above and left: McCall's Patterns, circa late 1960s. Homemade stuffed Poohs from McCall's patterns. Type of fabric, trim, and shirt varies greatly depending on individual taste, but all follow the McCall's pattern. Pattern is shown on left. Excellent condition pattern: $15-25.

Sears, circa late 1970s. Three different stitchery kits were available to make Pooh, Tigger or Eeyore. Shown are an unmade Tigger kit (left) and a finished Eeyore (right). Unmade kit in package: $35-45. Finished character: $15-25.

Gund for Sears, circa 1968 to 1978. Background, left to right: 11in (28cm) polyester Pooh with black plastic nose and eyes, made for bath time; 20in (51cm) gold plush Pooh with red felt shirt; 15in (38cm) gold plush Pooh with red felt shirt, pom-pom nose, plastic eyes. Foreground, left to right: 15in (38cm) gold plush Pooh with red felt shirt (talking version says: "You're my best friend" "I'm Winnie the Pooh," "When I run I huff and puff" and four other phrases); 10in (25cm) gold plush musical Pooh with red felt shirt. Excellent condition: $15-25. Talking Pooh in working condition: $45-65.

Gund for Sears, circa 1970 to 1983. Left to right: 13in (33cm) pink Piglet with red and white cotton sewn-in shirt, wearing red felt name banner; 7in (18cm) sitting Tigger; 14in (36cm) and 20in (51cm) standing Tiggers all orange and black with white trim. Another version of Tigger has a black plastic nose instead of pom-pom. Near mint condition Tigger: $15-25. Near mint condition Piglet: $30-45.

Gund for Sears, circa 1970s. Left to right: 8in (20cm) sitting Eeyore, gray and white with name on chest; 11in (28cm) standing Eeyore, gray and white; 13in (33cm) sitting Eeyore, gray and white; 9in (23cm) sitting Eeyore, gray and white; 8in (20cm) standing Eeyore, gray and white; and 8in (20cm) Eeyore, all gray. All Eeyores have paper eyes, black mane and tails. Excellent condition: $15-25. Excellent condition solid gray Eeyore: $25-40.

Animal Fair, circa 1970s. Gold and red plush Pooh handpuppet with pom-pom nose, black plastic eyes; orange, black and white plush

Tigger handpuppet, pom-pom nose, white and black plastic eyes. Very good condition: $20-40.

Made in Korea for Disney Parks, circa late 1970s. Left to right: 8in (20cm) blue and gray plush Eeyore; 7in (18cm) gold and red plush Pooh; 14in (36cm) gold and red plush Pooh; 12in (31cm) orange, black and white Tigger; 8in (20cm) two-tone gray Eeyore with bean-bag stuffing. Excellent condition: $20-35.

Anne Wilkerson, circa 1990s. Cloth, 3in (8cm) Pooh in pouch. Yellow and red colors and black features are printed on cloth. Mint condition: $15-25.

Anne Wilkerson, circa 1990s. Cloth pop-up toys of Pooh and Piglet. The character can be moved in and out of the cylinder or cone with the attached stick. Pooh is yellow with red shirt and Piglet is pink with a green and black shirt. All features and shirts are printed on character. Mint condition: $35-45.

Anne Wilkerson, circa 1981 to 1991. Left to right: 20in (51cm) quilted Pooh, 13in (33cm) Pooh, and 14in (36cm) Pooh. All are cotton with either a red cotton shirt or red felt vest. Facial features are painted. The cloth ball containing bell is held by the 20in (51cm) quilted Pooh. Near mint condition Poohs: $65-100. Mint condition Bell: $30-40.

Anne Wilkerson, circa late 1980s to 1990s. Left to right: 6in (15cm) cloth Pooh with red felt vest, orange and black Tigger, pink Piglet with green and black sewn-in shirt, and gray and blue Eeyore with black yarn mane. Mint condition: $35-50.

Anne Wilkerson, circa 1990s. Cloth, stuffed books of Pooh
and Piglet in closed position. Mint condition: $35-45.

Anne Wilkerson, circa 1990s. Cloth, stuffed books of Pooh and Piglet in open position. (Shown closed on previous page.) Mint condition: $35-45.

Anne Wilkerson, circa 1990. Cloth finger puppets on cards sold through The Disney Store. Set of four include: gold and black Tigger, gray Eeyore, pink Piglet with green and black shirt, and tan Pooh. Mint in package: $10-15.

Anne Wilkerson, circa late 1980s to 1990s. "Goodnight Pooh" 14in (36cm) gold cloth Pooh tucked into blue and white checkered bed. Matching slippers also available. Excellent condition Pooh: $35-50. Mint condition slippers: $25-35.

California Stuffed Toys, circa 1970s to 1980s. Two versions of the popular Grad Night Poohs sold at the Disney Parks on specially reserved Grad Nights. All have a sewn-in ribbon to designate the year, plus the smaller 15in (38cm) versions may have a black felt "mortarboard" hat (the hat on the 24in [61cm] Pooh pictured here is not original). Pin-back buttons were also available as displayed on the Pooh to the right. Excellent condition: $15-35.

Possibly Tokyo Disneyland, circa 1980s. Reinforced, 22in (56cm) Pooh with long beige fur, black plastic eyes, black leatherette nose with a bee nearby. The shirt is pink with white lettering. A copyright Walt Disney Productions tag is sewn into a leg. Although he was purchased in Guam, his body style and lettering on the shirt suggest a strong tie to Tokyo Disneyland in the early to mid 1980s. Excellent condition: $125-175.

John Adams Toy Company, England, circa 1983. **Below:** 25in (64cm) yellow plush Pooh with red felt shirt and red tag that reads "I'm Pooh," black glass eyes, pom-pom nose. **Opposite Page, Top:** 6in (15cm) fuzzy gold and black Tigger. A small Pooh, Piglet, and Eeyore were also manufactured, as well as 10in (25cm) to 18in (46cm) Pooh, Piglet, Kanga, Roo, Rabbit, Tigger, Eeyore, and Owl. "Sew Your Own" kits were made for Pooh, Tigger, Piglet, and Eeyore. All Characters, mint condition large, 25in (64cm) or medium, 10-18in (25-46cm): $100-150. Mint condition small, 6in (15cm) and kits: $35-50.

Made in Korea for Disney Parks, circa 1980 to 1988. Left to right: 7in (18cm) orange, black and light yellow Tigger, also in 14in (36cm) and 25in (64cm), 6in (15cm) pink Piglet with pink and black sewn-in shirt, gold plush 14in (36cm) Pooh with red velour shirt (7in [18cm] version found as well), 14in (36cm) brown and pink Kanga with Roo, 8in (20cm) two-tone blue Eeyore. Excellent condition: $15-35.

Above: R. John Wright, circa late 1980s. 8in (20cm) Piglet with a green shirt and life-sized Pooh, 18in (46cm) tan mohair with maroon vest. Limited editions of 2500 Poohs and 1000 Piglets. Mint in box Pooh: $600-800. Mint in box Piglet: $350-400.

Opposite Page: R. John Wright, circa 1987 to 1989. Pooh with honey pot, tan mohair, jointed with felt bee in ear, white cotton bib, and ceramic honey pot. Also available but not pictured was Piglet with violets. Mint in box Pooh: $400-500. Mint in box Piglet: $200-300. Value will probably rise in near future since this version was recently discontinued.

R. John Wright, circa 1980s. Left to right: 5in (13cm) pink felt Piglet with green and black shirt, 8in (20cm) tan mohair Pooh with maroon vest, 8in (20cm) mustard and black felt Tigger, 8in (20cm) brown and white plush Kanga with 3in (8cm) baby Roo, 10in (25cm) gray felt Eeyore, 18in (46cm) Christopher Robin II wearing rain gear and carrying umbrella. All dolls are jointed and made in limited editions of 500 for Christopher Robin; 1000 for Piglet, Eeyore, Kanga and Tigger; and 2500 for Pooh. Mint in box Pooh: $500-600. Mint in box Piglet, Tigger, Kanga/Roo, Eeyore: $350-500 each. Christopher Robin I or II (version I is without rain gear): $1300-1600.

R. John Wright, circa 1989. 10in (25cm) tan mohair Pooh, jointed with maroon vest in blue felt chair. Box is designed like a house. Limited edition of 500, sold at the Second Annual Teddy Bear Convention in Orlando, Florida. Mint in box: $750-850.

Gund for Sears, circa 1970 to 1983. Left to right: 8in (20cm) peach and blue Roo with brown pom-pom nose and name on chest; 10in (25cm) chubbier Pooh, gold plush with red shirt and name on front of shirt; 8in (20cm) musical version of Pooh with nondetachable shirt; 13in (33cm) peach and blue Roo, brown pom-pom nose and name on chest. Also available was 10in (25cm) Roo similar in style to the 13in (33cm) Roo only with stubby tail. Very good condition Roo or Pooh: $10-25.

Gund, circa 1986. Special centennial Pooh celebrating Sears 100th year anniversary. Pooh is jointed, gold plush with a red sweater shirt with patch on left arm. Mint in box: $100-150.

Tokyo Disneyland, circa 1988 to 1990. Left to right: 18in (46cm) sitting Pooh, gold plush, red shirt with name and bee on chest, black pom-pom nose and plastic eyes; 12in (31cm) sitting Pooh with stuffed honey pot on head, gold plush with name on red shirt and black velvet nose; 14in (36cm) standing Eeyore, blue and gray with prominent black stitching; 18in (46cm) sitting Pooh, gold plush red shirt and brown leather nose; 8in (20cm) sitting Pooh with bee on face and red shirt inscribed with name; 20in (51cm) Tigger, orange, black and white with a black leather nose and black plastic eyes. Large mint condition Poohs: $80-125. Mint condition Eeyore or Tigger: $75-100. Mint condition 8in (20cm) Pooh: $30-45.

Tokyo Disneyland, circa 1989. A complete set of plush from Japan that was also available at the Japanese Showcase in Epcot Center, Orlando, Florida. Includes a 13in (33cm) brown and pink Kanga with tan and blue Roo in pouch, 14in (36cm) Tigger, 9in (23cm) two-tone blue Eeyore, 13in (33cm) Pooh with brown leather nose and red shirt, 8in (20cm) pink Piglet with purple scarf, 11in (28cm) brown and beige Owl, 11in (28cm) yellow and white Rabbit. Mint condition: $40-75.

Tokyo Disneyland, circa 1990 to 1992. Plush musical Poohs include 6in (15cm) sitting and 10in (25cm) standing Pooh. Both are yellow with red shirts and head moves from side to side as Pooh theme song plays. Standing Pooh available at EPCOT'S Japanese Pavilion. Mint condition: $50-75.

Caltoy, Inc. and TCA Group, circa 1988 to 1989. Group of "Poohfessionals" sold by Sears. Back row (left to right): include: Bedtime Pooh, Pooh for President, Soldier Pooh, Football Player Pooh, Front row (left to right): Doctor Pooh, Hollywood Pooh, Wizard Pooh, Tuxedo Pooh, and Backpacker Pooh. 9in (23cm) to 14in (36cm). Mint condition: $25-35.

Tokyo Disneyland, circa 1990. More plush varieties from left to right: standing and sitting 7in (18cm) Pooh; 12in (31cm) Pooh with bee on face next to nose. All Poohs are wearing red shirts with inscribed names; 9in (23cm) Tigger, orange, black and white with black leather nose. Mint condition small Poohs and small Tigger: $30-45. Mint condition 12in (31cm) Pooh: $50-65.

Tokyo Disneyland, circa 1990. Peach and brown 14in (36cm) Kanga with long eyelashes and baby Roo in pocket. Mint condition Kanga/Roo: $45-60.

Sears, circa 1988 to 1990. Left to right: 10in (25cm) gold plush Pooh with red sweater shirt with name on it; 8in (20cm) orange, black and white Tigger with curly tail; 8in (20cm) two-tone blue Eeyore; and 11in (28cm) gold plush Pooh with red sweater shirt with name containing musical disk. Mint condition: $15-25.

Sears, circa 1988 to 1990. Left to right: 10in (25cm) gold plush Pooh with open red vest; 8in (20cm) pink Piglet; 12in (31cm) standing Tigger, orange and black with yellow belly; and 9in (23cm) gray and pink Eeyore with black stitching on face. Mint condition: $15-25.

TCA Group for Sears, circa 1989 to 1990. To augment the opening of "The New Adventures of Winnie the Pooh," small 5in (13cm) to 6in (15cm) plush became available through Sears as "Disney's Classic Plush." The coverings on all are a polyester blend, all have plastic eyes. Mint in box: $10-20.

Sears, circa 1989 to 1990. Left to right: unusual 11in (28cm) sitting Pooh yellow plush with red shirt and name, 11in (28cm) Lovenotes Pooh musical gold plush Pooh with red sweater and name, 6in (15cm) gold plush Pooh with red sweater, 11in (28cm) gold plush Pooh with printed name on red sweater and arms held up, 8in (20cm) gold plush Pooh with red fuzzy "shirt" (shirt is sewn into body). Mint condition: $10-25.

McDonald's and Sears, circa 1987 to 1989. Pooh character plush used as premiums. Left to right: 8in (20cm) Eeyore, gray and white; Pooh, gold with name printed on red shirt; and Tigger, orange, black and beige that were available at only 75 McDonald's res-taurants in the Midwest. To right is a 6in (15cm) plush Pooh with a red shirt available at Sears with a coupon from Honey Nut Cheerios. Excellent condition McDonald plush: $35-45. 6in (15cm) Pooh from Sears: $10.

Canasa Trading Corp., circa 1988. The Pooh mascot of the First Annual Teddy Bear Convention in Orlando, Florida. 20in (51cm) Pooh is gold plush with red and white winter hat and scarf with Teddy Bear Convention pin attached to scarf. Mint condition: $75-125.

Circa 1989 to 1990. Set of Eeyore, Tigger and Pooh available at Sears for a nominal cost. Size is 5in (13cm) to 6in (15cm), all are plush covered. Mint condition: $5.

Canasa Trading Corp., circa 1989 to 1990. Set of Pooh character plush available at Disney Parks and Stores. Left to right: brown and pink Kanga, 16in (41cm); brown 9in (23cm) Roo wearing blue shirt; 24in (61cm) jointed gold with name printed on red shirt Pooh; 9in (23cm) pink Piglet; 18in (46cm) orange, black, and yellow Tigger in bouncing position; and 8in (20cm) sitting gray and white Eeyore. Mint condition: $15-30.

Sears, circa 1989. Giant gold plush Pooh wearing red knit sweater with embossed name. Measures 31in (79cm) from head to rump. Each Sears store across the country awarded one of these Poohs to the winner of a drawing held in December 1989 as a Christmas promotion. Mint condition: $200-250.

Playskool United Kingdom, circa 1991.
Plush 7in (18cm) yellow Pooh with red shirt
sold at Harrods. "Winnie" is painted on shirt.
Mint condition: $35-40.

Sears, Canada, circa 1980s. Gold plush 14in (36cm) and 12in (31cm) Poohs. Red shirts vary from velveteen (left) to polyester (middle) to felt (right) but all have embossed name across their chests. Canada Pooh is characterized by the external tongue, black plastic eyes and black yarn mouth and nose. Excellent condition: $25-40.

Ceramic Pooh and Friends

Richard Krueger, Germany, circa 1950s. Ceramic mug depicting Christopher Robin nailing Eeyore's tail while Pooh watches. Same picture is on both sides. Very good condition: $50-60.

Enesco, circa mid-1960s. Three versions of the larger 4in (10cm) to 5in (13cm) Winnie the Pooh which includes: Pooh sitting on a clump of grass, waving; Pooh walking on a clump of grass; and Pooh sitting on a log, waving. Bottoms are marked "Walt Disney Productions Japan," and sometimes bear the stamp MCMLXIV (1964). Enesco ceramics were sold at Disneyland at an original price of $1.00 each. Pooh possesses eyelashes on all Enesco versions, and is gold with a red shirt. Excellent condition: $50-75.

Enesco, circa mid-1960s. The remainder of the Enesco Pooh characters include: 5in (13cm) yellow and black sitting Tigger, 3in (8cm) high blue-gray Eeyore with white muzzle and black mane (Eeyore also has a leather tail tacked to his body), 5in (13cm) brown and beige Owl, 5in (13cm) Christopher Robin playing a snare drum and wearing a yellow shirt and dark blue shorts, 5in (13cm) brown and salmon Kanga with Roo in pouch, and 5in (13cm) yellow and white Rabbit. Bottoms are marked as described for Pooh above. There are at least two other color versions of Eeyore. One shows Eeyore with a white mane. The other has Eeyore painted a pale blue (including muzzle) with a black mane. Pieces originally included a gold paper tag around the necks marked Winnie the Pooh" with the character's name on the inside. Excellent condition: $75-125.

Enesco, circa mid-1960s. Four versions of the smaller Pooh include: 4in (10cm) Pooh standing on one foot holding balloon, 4in (10cm) Pooh standing, holding balloon, 4in (10cm) Pooh sitting on a log holding a balloon marked "Pooh For President," 3½in (9cm) Pooh in sprawled sitting position holding balloon. (The balloon pictured here may not be original.) For all versions, Pooh is gold with a red shirt and balloons are blue styrofoam often atoped with a bee. The Pooh sitting on a log is more commonly found without a "Pooh For President" banner, and should then be priced in the lower range. Pieces were sold originally with a gold paper tag around the necks marked "Winnie the Pooh." Excellent condition. Pooh For President, Pooh on one foot: $70-100. Standing Pooh, Pooh sprawled: $25-40.

Enesco, circa mid-1960s. Left to right: Pencil holder and sharpener in brown tones, with Pooh standing to the side, 4½in (12cm); 8in (20cm) Pooh cookie jar in brown tones with a gold Pooh wearing a red shirt; 4½in (12cm) bank in brown tones with a gold Pooh wearing a red shirt. Excellent condition. Pencil holder: $45-55. Cookie jar: $125-200. Bank: $25-35.

Enesco, circa mid-1960s. Two sets of salt and pepper shakers. One set consists of Pooh and Rabbit. Pooh is gold with a red shirt and Rabbit is yellow and white. Both are 4in (10cm) in height. The other set is Kanga and Roo. Excellent condition: $100-150.

Winnie the Pooh
and Friends

Above: Mug — Keele St. Pty. Company, England, circa 1965. Plate — Disneyland, circa 1964. Mug pictures Pooh and Piglet in very fat condition, eating honey. On back of mug is a small picture of Pooh sitting with honey pot (right). Mug is labeled "Winnie the Pooh and Piglet." Plate pictures Pooh, Eeyore, Piglet, Rabbit, Kanga, Roo, Owl, Gopher, Tigger and Christopher Robin and is labeled "Winnie the Pooh and Friends." A 1964 copyright is on the back of the plate. Excellent condition. Mug: $50-60. Plate: $85-125.

Disneyland, circa 1964. Mugs featuring Pooh and Rabbit. Both characters are in relief with Pooh holding a blue balloon and labeled "Winnie-the-Pooh's mug." Both have a 1964 copyright on bottom. Very good condition: $30-45 each.

Disney Parks (Made in Japan), circa late 1960s to early 1970s. Left: 6in (15cm) ceramic honey holder dividing Pooh into two pieces. Pooh is yellow with a red shirt and holding a brown honey pot. On the back is a notch for a honey spoon. Right: 6in (15cm) bank of a gold Pooh with red shirt and blue honey pot. Excellent condition: $25-35 each.

Disney Parks (Made in Japan), circa early 1970s. Left: 6in (15cm) composition Pooh nodder sitting on green base. Right: 6in (15cm) composition Pooh bank. Both Poohs are orange-gold in color with a red shirt. Near mint condition: $25-40.

Sears, circa 1970s. Glossy ceramic bookends of yellow Rabbit pushing gold Pooh through the door to Rabbit's house. A similar set was produced by Enesco in the 1960s that shows Rabbit pushing Pooh out the door while Christopher Robin is pulling on Pooh from the other side. Near mint condition: $75-100.

Beswick, England, circa late 1960s to present. Left to right: 3in (8cm) brown and white Owl; 3in (8cm) brown and tan Kanga; 2½in (4cm) gold Pooh with red shirt; 2½in (4cm) pink Piglet wearing red shirt; 5in (13cm) Christopher Robin carrying books and apple, wearing a yellow shirt and navy shorts; 3in (8cm) tan and white Rabbit; 3in (8cm) yellow and black Tigger; 2½in (6cm) gray Eeyore. Bottoms are marked "Beswick England." These are fairly common due to the extended length of production. Mint condition: $30-50.

Above and Below: Disney Parks and Sears, circa 1970s. Left to right: ceramic mug with all the Pooh characters pictured, made in Japan and sold at the Disney Parks. Another view is shown in the illustration below, left Middle: ceramic mug sold through Sears with Pooh and Owl in relief and Tigger as the handle. Right: ceramic mug sold through Sears showing Pooh handing a balloon to Piglet, causing Piglet to float away. A different view is shown below, right. Near mint condition: $25-40 each.

Sears, circa mid-1970s. Ceramic purple honey pot" planter with yellow and white Rabbit on one side, and gold Pooh wearing red shirt on the other. Near mint condition: $65-85.

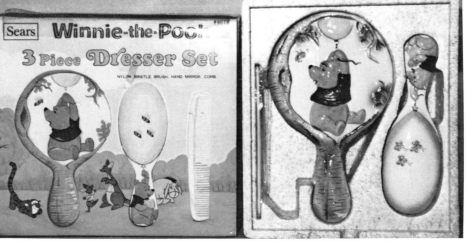

Sears, circa mid-1970s. Three-piece dresser set consisting of a plastic comb, a ceramic mirror with Pooh holding a blue balloon next to a brown tree in relief on the back of the mirror, and a ceramic brush with Pooh holding a blue balloon and bees nearby. Mint in box: $95-115.

Sears, circa mid-1970s. Left: 12in (31cm) Tigger cookie jar, orange with black stripes and white muzzle and eye area. Tigger's head comprises the lid of the jar, and he is "holding" a ceramic basket inscribed "Cookies." Another color version of Tigger can be found where the "basket" is painted yellow. Right: 10in (25cm) tall Eeyore cookie jar. Eeyore is gray with blue ears, muzzle, tail and underside of legs. The lid is the pink bow at the end of the tail (on his back, in this position). His mane is black and eyes are black on a white background. Excellent condition Tigger: $145-200. Eeyore: $195-250.

Sears, circa 1970s. 11in (28cm) commonly found Pooh cookie jar which shows a yellow Pooh wearing a red shirt and holding a blue honey pot. A bee is on Pooh's head and his head serves as the lid to the jar. Also a 10in (25cm) Pooh cookie jar depicting a smaller Pooh holding a large hunny pot. Pooh is yellow with a red shirt. The pot is two-toned brown with a bee on top. The lid of the hunny pot is the lid to the cookie jar. Near mint condition: $75-125.

A rare Pooh cookie jar (*from the collection of Lisa Walshe*) in which Pooh is holding a honey pot on top of his head. Top of head removes. *Photograph is courtesy of Lisa Walshe*. Mint condition Pooh with pot on head: $125-200.

Made in Japan, circa mid-1970s. Tigger is part of a set of Pooh ceramics sold at Sears. Each are close to 2in (5cm) tall. Shown are Pooh, gold with red shirt and eating out of honey pot; and Tigger, orange with black stripes and white belly and muzzle. No shown are: Owl, Kanga, Rabbit, Piglet Eeyore. Excellent condition: $20-25 each.

'okyo Disneyland, Sears, circa mid-1970s o 1990. Left to right: 6in (15cm) ceramic ank sold through Tokyo Disneyland in 990. Pooh is sitting outside the door to is tree house with a honey pot in hand. in (15cm) bank sold through Sears in he mid-1970s. Pooh's house is more fully formed, and Pooh is standing near the door. Sears mid-1970s 7in (18cm) ceramic nightlight shaped like a mushroom with Pooh, Tigger, Rabbit, and Eeyore sleeping underneath. Mint condition. Tokyo bank: $75-100. Sears bank: $75-110. Mushroom nightlight: $50-125.

Sears, circa mid-1970s to 1987. Left to right: Musical jewelry box composed of cardboard. The outer cover is a black and white map of the 100 Acre Wood, the inside contains colorful pictures of Pooh and his house. Sold through Sears in the mid-1970s. A musical snowglobe of Pooh with a basket. Pictured on the base are Eeyore, Rabbit and Tigger. Sold through Sears in 1987. Right is a combination, musical, snowglobe, kaleidoscope. Within the clear casing are Tigger, Eeyore, Pooh, Rabbit and Piglet. These figures rotate while music is played. One can look through the kaleidoscope and disrupt the "snow" for an even greater effect. Sold through Sears in 1987. Near mint condition. Cardboard jewelry box: $45-$55. Snowglobe: $50-65. Kaleidoscope: $50-65.

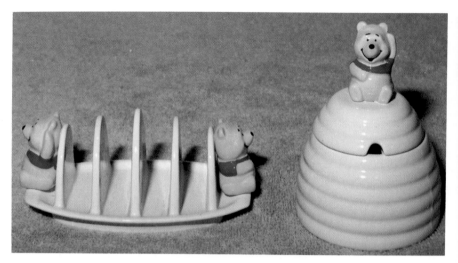

Wayman Ceramics, circa 1980s. Left is a 7in (18cm) long napkin holder with Pooh seated at both ends. Right is a 6in (15cm) honey pot in the shape of a beehive with Pooh seated at top. Both pieces are predominately white while Pooh is yellow with a red shirt. Near mint condition: $50-65 each.

Made in Japan, circa 1980s. A set of ceramics sold at the Disney Parks and Stores that included: 3in (8cm) tall gray and white Eeyore with black mane and tail (note the similar pose to the 1960s Enesco Eeyore, but the current Eeyore has a tail formed as part of the ceramic figure), 4in (10cm) orange and black Tigger with a white face and belly, and 4in (10cm) gold Pooh with red shirt pulling sticky honey from pot. There was a set issued in the 1970s, utilizing the same molds, but with muted colors. Mint condition: $5-8 each.

Schmid, circa early 1980s. Schimd musicals were made in Japan and characterized by figures on a ceramic round base atop a smaller plastic round base which winds to play the song and rotate the figures. Musical of Eeyore and Pooh with honey pots. *Photograph courtesy of Lisa Walshe.* Near mint condition: $75-125.

Schmid musicals, circa early 1980s, made in Japan, are characterized by figures on a ceramic round base atop a smaller plastic round base which winds to play the song and rotate the figures. Shown are Pooh and Rabbit who rotate to the tune of "Zipadee Do Dah," Kanga and Roo to "It's a Small World," and Pooh on a swing with Rabbit and Owl nearby to the theme from Winnie the Pooh. Not pictured are Pooh and Christopher Robin, Pooh and Tigger, and Pooh and Piglet. Near mint condition: $75-125.

Sears, circa 1987. Set of three tiny ceramics about 1½in (4cm) tall: orange and black Tigger with white face and belly, gray and white Eeyore with black mane, and gold Pooh with honey pot on head and red shirt. Mint condition: $5 each.

Grolier, circa 1980s. Bisque, 2in (5cm) Pooh, yellow with red shirt, eating honey from pot; and 3in (8cm) bisque Tigger, orange and black with white belly and face. Could only be purchased from Grolier as part of a set of Disney characters. Mint condition: $25-40 each.

Tokyo Disneyland, circa late 1980s. Left to right: 3in (8cm) gold Pooh with red shirt and honey pot on head; 3in (8cm) gold Pooh playing musical instrument and wearing red shirt, sitting on orange base (part of a set of Disney characters playing musical instruments); 2in (5cm) gold Pooh sitting on log, pointing in air (popular Japanese pose) wearing red shirt; and 2in (5cm) gold Pooh with red shirt eating honey out of pot. Mint condition: $20-35.

Sears, circa 1987. Left is a 7in (18cm) ceramic bank of Pooh sitting on an overturned honey pot. Pot is brown and white. Pooh is yellow with a red shirt. Right is a ceramic musical of Pooh eating honey on a stump. The stump is brown with lavender flowers at base, honey pot is two-toned brown, and Pooh is yellow with a red shirt. The musical plays the theme to "Winnie the Pooh." Mint condition. Bank: $25-35. Musical: $35-45.

Choose any of your favorite characters
or collect the complete scene.

Willitts, circa 1989. A set of 12 bisque pieces that comprise the scene of the 100 Acre Woods. The figures are about 3in (8cm) tall and consist of: Piglet sitting on a stump, Rabbit, Kanga and Roo, Eeyore, Tigger, Owl, Pooh, Christopher Robin and four pieces that make up the log in the background. The set was available with a wooden tray to hold the pieces. This set is pictured with the dealer's display. Mint condition: $250-300 set.

Unknown, circa 1980s. Set of three snowglobes labeled "Magic Kingdom Collection," featuring Eeyore, Pooh and Tigger. The ceramic figures within the globe are identical to the three tiny ceramic figures sold by Sears in 1987. The base of the globes is wood. They are not musical. Near mint condition: $70 each.

Willitts, circa 1988-1989. Bisque musical figurines from left to right: Christopher Robin nailing Eeyore's tail while Pooh watches, entitled "I have my friends. Someone spoke to me only yesterday." Gifts are given with Owl, Kanga, Roo, Pooh, Piglet and Christopher Robin present, entitled "Three cheers for Pooh." Pooh lifts a honey pot from a basket while Piglet watches, entitled "When you're rumbly in your tumbly." Mint condition: $70-100.

Willitts, circa 1988-1989. Bisque musical figurines of Pooh writing (Love from Pooh) and Pooh standing by the North Pole sign (The Exposition). Mint condition: $35-50.

Above and Below: Willitts, circa 1988 to 1989. Six bisque figurines about 2in (5cm) to 3in (8cm) tall, left to right: Pooh writing, Pooh and Piglet on log inscribed "It's so much friendlier with two," Pooh holding candle. Below: Pooh bathing, Pooh sitting on basket reading "The Love of Honey," and Pooh watching honey pour from log. Pooh is pale yellow with maroon shirt (except bathing Pooh who has no shirt). Mint condition: $15-25.

Villitts, circa 1988-1989. Left to right: bisque Pooh bank, bisque Pooh bell, bisque potpourri container with Pooh sitting in front of house, bisque planter of Pooh climbing tree house. Also made was a potpourri holder identical to the bisque bell shown second from left. Mint condition: $30-70.

Charpente, circa 1989-1990. Bisque bookends of Rabbit and his friend helping Christopher Robin pull Pooh out of Rabbit's house. Mint condition: $60-70.

Willitts, circa 1988-1989. Smaller bisque musicals from top to bottom: Pooh and Owl "To an astute and helpful bear;" Pooh and Eeyore, "Having a smackeral of something;" Pooh in snow, "Tracking a wozzle wasn' hard for a bear of little brain." Mint condition: $35-50.

Willitts, circa 1988-1989. Left: musical snowglobe of Pooh and honey pot entitled "Sing Ho for the life of a Pooh." Right: ceramic potpourri container with Pooh and Piglet pictured on bottom section. Mint condition: $50-75.

Tokyo Disneyland, circa 1989-1990. Left to right: Ceramic pencil holder with Pooh in relief holding pink and blue mouse-ears balloons. Ceramic musical that also rotates with Pooh balancing honey pot on head. Large ceramic musical honey pot containing Pooh moving in and out of the honey pot. The other Pooh characters are pictured along the bottom of the pot. Mint condition. Pencil holder/small musical: $40-55. Musical honey pot: $75-100.

Disney Parks and Stores, circa 1990. Left: musical of Pooh and Piglet placing blocks atop one another. Right: Pooh bank. Mint condition. Musical: $45. Bank: $25.

Reed and Barton, circa 1990. Ceramic dish and metal flatware set for children. Utensils include Eeyore on fork, Pooh on spoon, and Piglet on spoon. Dish set includes a drinking cup with Rabbit looking at Pooh stuck in his door; a plate with Tigger falling out of a tree towards Christopher Robin, Piglet, Pooh, Eeyore, and Roo; and a bowl with Christopher Robin, Pooh and Piglet having a picnic. Mint condition: $40 set.

Tokyo Disneyland, circa 1990. Dish set that includes a mug and saucer, plate, bowl, mug, cup, creamer, bell, and sugar container. Each pictures a different scene with Pooh and Piglet, except for the bell which features a figural ceramic Pooh as the bell handle. Mint condition: $100-125 set.

Disney Parks and Stores, circa 1990. Three glossy ceramic picture frames from left to right: rectangle frame with Tigger above Pooh's doorway (next to "Mr. Sanders" sign) and Pooh below standing with honey pot, double oval frame with Tigger, Eeyore, Piglet and Pooh in relief, and single oval frame with Tigger above in tree and Pooh below sitting with honey pot. Mint condition: $25-35 each.

Disney Parks and Stores, circa 1990. Ceramic bookends featuring Piglet catching falling books and Pooh balancing honey pots. Mint condition: $50.

Disney Parks and Stores, circa 1990 to 1991. Left to right: orange and black Tigger with yellow face and belly, two-toned gray Eeyore with pink ear lining and black mane, gold Pooh with red shirt and brown honey pot, and pink Piglet with dark pink shirt. All stand about 4in (10cm). Mint condition: $5-8.

Disney Parks, circa 1990 to 1991. Set of 6in (15cm) ceramic figures that serve as hangers. Left to right: gray Eeyore with black mane, gold Pooh with red shirt, pink Piglet with dark pink shirt, and orange and black Tigger with yellow face and belly. Mint condition: $10 each.

Willitts, circa 1990-1991. Animated, musical bisque figurines of Pooh atop Tigger "When you're rumbly in you tumbly" which moves Pooh and Tigger towards and away from honey pot, and Pooh rolling on back with honey pot that moves back and forth "Silly old bear. How I do love you." Mint condition: $70-100.

Willitts, circa 1990-1991. Bisque, musical figurines from left to right: Pooh and Piglet in snow, "Say you like it because it's yours, because I love you!"; Christopher Robin reading to Pooh who is stuck in Rabbit's door, "Some words to comfort a wedged bear in great tightness...I love you."; Pooh trying mathematics, "A bear of enormous brain." Mint condition: $35-70 each.

Willitts, circa 1990 to 1991. Left to right: pink Piglet with green shirt, carrying balloon; orange and brown Tigger eating honey; pink Piglet with green shirt holding flowers; yellow Pooh with red shirt and blue honey pot stuck on head, Piglet nearby. All figures are bisque and are 2in (5cm) to 3in (8cm) tall. Mint condition: $10-15 each.

Left and Below: Willitts, circa 1990 to 1991. Left: yellow Pooh wearing red shirt peering into blue honey pot and gray Eeyore standing on head with real pink ribbon tied to tail. Below: pink Piglet wearing green shirt, writing; orange and brown Tigger in flower bed. All are bisque and range from 2in (5cm) to 3in (8cm) in height. Mint condition: $10-15 each.

Willitts, circa 1990 to 1991. Musical snowglobes of Piglet holding flowers "Because Spring is really springing"; Piglet next to Pooh, honey jar stuck on Pooh's head "It all comes from liking honey too much"; Tigger bouncing in flowers "Bouncing is what Tiggers do best"; and Piglet holding balloon "Nobody can be uncheered by a balloon." The bases are a rough ceramic to provide a wooden appearance. Mint condition: $50-75 each.

Willitts, circa 1990-1991. Bisque figural nightlights of Pooh (yellow with maroon shirt), Piglet (pink with green shirt), and Tigger (yellow with brown stripes). Mint condition: $40-60 each.

Willitts, circa 1990-1991. Bisque banks including Tigger sniffing flowers and Piglet holding a balloon. Mint condition: $30-45 each.

Charpente, circa 1989 to 1991. Glossy ceramic tray set with matching mug. Mug has tiny ceramic Pooh sitting within. Mint condition. Tray set of three pieces: $40-45. Mint condition. Mug: $15-25.

Charpente, circa 1989-1991. Glossy ceramic picture frames and light switch plate featuring Pooh and Christopher Robin. Mint in box: $20-40.

The Disney Store, circa 1991. With the arrival of "Pooh Month" (January 1991) at The Disney Store, came a wealth of Pooh collectibles. Included are left to right: 2in (5cm) pink Piglet holding red heart; 3in (8cm) two-toned gray Eeyore holding red kite; 8in (20cm) gold musical Pooh with red shirt next to pink Piglet in basket holding balloons; 3in (8cm) orange and black Tigger with yellow face and belly, wearing blue cap and holding a blue mouse-ears balloon; 3in (8cm) gold Pooh with red shirt and blue and white checkered bib, holding honey pot. All are bisque, made in Japan. Mint condition. Figures: $8-14 each. Mint condition. Musical: $50-60.

The Disney Store, circa 1991. Making their debut during "Pooh Month" at The Disney Store. Above (from left to right): candy dish with Pooh and purple balloon on lid; candy dish without lid with Pooh holding balloon in relief on sides. Below (from left to right): oval picture frame with Pooh and Piglet holding purple, blue and yellow balloons; rectangular picture frame with Pooh and Piglet riding in basket, holding pastel balloons. Mint condition: $20-40.

Top and Bottom: The Disney Store, circa 1991. Ceramic mugs in both Disney and classic style. Mint condition: $5-8.

Japan, circa 1991. Glossy ceramic musicals. Left to right: 5in (13cm) Pooh playing horn from Tokyo Disneyland, 5in (13cm) Pooh on balloon and 8in (20cm) standing Pooh both from EPCOT'S Japanese Pavilion. All play the Pooh theme song. Mint condition: $50-75 each.

Willitts, circa 1991. 7in (18cm) bisque sculpture of Pooh and his tree house with friends Piglet, Kanga and Tigger. Mint in box: $65-80.

Plastic, Vinyl and Wooden Figurines

Nabisco, circa 1964-1965. Plastic, 2in (5cm) Pooh pals found as cereal premiums in boxes of Wheat Honeys or Rice Honeys. Left to right: Eeyore, Owl, Rabbit, Pooh, Christopher Robin, Piglet, and Kanga were available. (Tigger was not included). The arms are bent to allow the figurines to hang from cereal bowls, and each figurine also has a slot on its bottom to allow it to ride on a spoon (hence the term spoonrider is often used for these figurines). Beware of copies, they are literally a dime a dozen. The originals have a copyright symbol on their bellies that says "Walt Disney Productions" "1964." Copies have no such symbol but may have a slightly raised area in its place where the symbol was blotted out in manufacturing. Excellent condition. Original, copyrighted: $15-20 each.

Holland Hall, circa 1966. Vinyl squeeze toys from left to right: 7in (18cm) yellow and black Tigger, 7in (18cm) brown and tan Kanga and Roo, 13in (33cm) jointed yellow Pooh with red shirt, 4in (10cm) blue Eeyore, and 5in (13cm) yellow Pooh with red shirt licking honey from pot. One distinctive feature of Holland Hall vinyls is the "stitch" marks etched along the seam lines to make the figure appear as a stuffed animal. Excellent condition. Small set: $20-25 each. Large Pooh: $40-45.

Bendy and Ideal, circa late 1960s. Left: 12in (31cm) foam rubber Christopher Robin made by Ideal in Japan. Right: 7in (18cm) foam rubber Pooh made by Bendy in England.

Due to the fragility of these products, few are found in better than good condition. Good condition: $35-50 each.

Marx, circa late 1960s. Hard plastic, 6in (15cm) Pooh (gold with red shirt) that moves when wound, and 4in (10cm) by 7in (18cm) hard plastic Eeyore with vinyl trim that hops when pumped. Excellent condition: $45-55 each.

Mattel, Disneyland, Sears, circa late 1960s to 1970s. Left: 6in (15cm) hard plastic Pooh talker by Mattel (1970s). Pooh is yellow with a red shirt. When string on back is pulled, the upper section of his head moves as he talks. Pooh's voice is realistic, following the style displayed in the animated featurettes. Middle: 7in (18cm) hard plastic Pooh transistor radio. Yellow Pooh with red shirt is sitting on a brown stump holding a purple honey pot. Made in Hong Kong and sold at Disneyland. Right: 7in (18cm) hard plastic radio in shape of Pooh's head. Made by Sears. Excellent condition. Pooh Talker: $45-55. Pooh Radio, working: $45-55.

Nabisco, circa 1966. Plastic, 12in (31cm) tall cereal containers in the shape of either Kanga and Roo, or Pooh. Kanga is blue-gray with a pink belly, and Pooh is gold with a red shirt. Both have screw caps on the bottom labeled "Nabisco Puppets Wheat Cereal." The figures could be used as (rather stiff) hand puppets when the lid is left off, or a slot could be cut in the back for a bank. Excellent condition: $35-45.

Chein, circa 1964. Musical ferris wheel with six plastic figures (left) in original box (below). Tin litho and plastic wheel revolves and plays "You Are My Sunshine." Figures include Pooh, Christopher Robin, Rabbit, Tigger, Kanga, and Eeyore. Mint in box: $150-250.

Sears, circa mid-1970s. A set of 2½in (6cm) plastic finger puppets sold through Sears in the mid-1970s, including Piglet (pink and black), Tigger (orange and black), Eeyore (two-tone blue), Pooh (yellow with red shirt) and Owl (brown and tan). Mint in box: $40. Separately, no box: $5-8 each.

Shelcore, circa mid-1970s. Vinyl squeeze toys, 7in (18cm) tall. Left to right: Pooh with rotating head and arms at sides, Tigger with rotating head and arms in air, Pooh with fused legs and waving, and Tigger with fused head and arms held high. The two figures with rotating heads are made of a harder vinyl. Excellent condition: $10-15 each.

Sears, circa late 1960s. Left to right: Hard 4in (10cm) vinyl gold Pooh with red shirt sold in the late 1960s with the Horsman Christopher Robin doll. Soft vinyl 4in (10cm) yellow Pooh with red shirt and green honey pot from 1987 to present. Soft vinyl 5in (13cm) Pooh wearing red nightshirt and cap, holding a white toothbrush from 1989 to present. Gray vinyl 7in (18cm) long Eeyore, made in Japan, probably from late 1960s. Very good condition, hard vinyl Pooh: $15-25. Mint condition, soft vinyl Poohs: $4-8. Very good condition, Eeyore: $15-30.

Shelcore, circa mid-1970s. Vinyl, two-part figure of Pooh holding honey pot and waving, mounted in plastic stump for battery-operated nightlight. Sold through Sears. This same figure was also utilized as a center piece of a mobile, and sold separately as a squeeze toy. Excellent condition. Figure: $8-12. Nightlight: $25-35.

Sears, circa late 1960s-1970s. Sears vinyl squeeze toys were produced in three different sizes: 8in (20cm), 6in (15cm), and 4in (10cm), and include a gold and red Pooh, brown Kanga with Baby Roo, pink Piglet with burgundy shirt, orange and black Tigger, and blue Eeyore. Very good condition, 8in (20cm) and 6in (15cm): $12-18. Very good condition, 4in (10cm): $5 each.

Hallmark, circa 1970s. Three different types of Pooh candles from left to right: 7in (18cm) figural Pooh candle, 4in (10cm) clay Pooh holding brown honey pot that serves as candle holder, and 2in (5cm) candle of a sitting Pooh holding honey pot, wrapped in cellophane. Excellent condition: $15-30 each.

56 Concepts Inc., circa 1970s. Set of 2in (5cm) high Pooh character erasers including Kanga with Roo, Piglet, Owl, Rabbit, Christopher Robin, Tigger, Eeyore, and Pooh. The Walt Disney copyright should be displayed on either the back or bottom of each. Once again beware, as unauthorized copies can be found and are not worth nearly as much. If the eraser is in decent condition and an original, the copyright should still be legible. Excellent condition: $5-8.

Sears and Tokyo Disneyland, circa 1970s. Left to right: Hard vinyl 6in (15cm) bank with one jointed arm and head, by Tokyo Disneyland 1989 to 1991. 8in (20cm) and 11in (28cm) hard vinyl banks sold through Sears in the 1970s. Mint condition, Tokyo bank: $25-35. Excellent condition, Sears banks: $20-30.

Sears, circa 1970s to 1980s. Vinyl squeeze toys left to right: 5in (13cm) Pooh sitting and eating honey, made in Taiwan, 1970s; 8in (20cm) jointed Pooh with cloth shirt, made in Japan, 1970s; 7in (18cm) Tigger holding his tail sold through Sears in the late 1980s; 7in (18cm) Pooh holding blue honey pot sold through Sears in the late 1980s. Excellent condition. Taiwanese and Japanese made vinyls: $10-18 each. Sears: $5-8 each.

Tokyo Disneyland, circa 1988 to 1989. Flocked, jointed vinyls of 3in (8cm) Piglet, pink with red shirt; 4in (10cm) Kanga, brown and tan; and 4in (10cm) Pooh, yellow with red shirt. Mint in box: $35-45 each.

Sears, circa 1987 to 1988. Jointed, 2in (5cm) hard plastic figures of Eeyore (blue and white), Pooh (yellow with red shirt), and Tigger (orange and black with white face and belly). Part of a Magic Kingdom set. Mint condition: $10-15 set.

Spain, circa 1988 to 1991. Hard vinyl 2in (5cm) figures of Pooh, gold with a red shirt. One Pooh is holding a blue honey pot, the other is waving. Mint condition: $10-15 each.

Made in England, circa 1980s. A set of 2in (5cm) to 3in (8cm) jointed, painted wooden figures of Eeyore, Rabbit, Owl, Kanga, Roo, Christopher Robin, Tigger, Piglet, and Pooh. Mint condition: $175-250 set.

Unknown, circa 1987 to 1989. Rubber 1½in (4cm) Pooh figurine from Belgium. Pooh is tan with black and white features, wearing either a blue or red shirt and holding a honey pot labeled "honig." Good condition: $15 each.

Bully, Germany, circa 1989 to present. Hard vinyl 2in (5cm) figurines of (top) pink Piglet standing on block; gold Pooh with red shirt waving; gray Eeyore; (below) orange, black and yellow Tigger; Pooh standing and waving, with honey pot; yellow and white Rabbit; and brown and pink Kanga with Roo. Mint condition: $8-15.

Sears and The Disney Store, circa 1989 to 1990. Wooden marionettes of Owl, Kanga, Eeyore, Rabbit, Tigger, Piglet, Pooh, Christopher Robin and Roo. Pooh could be purchased with stage. The other characters were sold as part of a pair. Mint in box: $15-25 each. Mint in box Stage: $50.

Sears, circa 1989 to 1990. Set of three hard vinyl figurines of Pooh (tan and red) holding honey pot and spoon, pink Piglet, and orange, black and tan Tigger holding megaphone. Mint condition: $15-25 set.

Disney Stores, circa 1990 to 1991. Set of 5in (13cm) vinyl squeeze toys sold in clear plastic case. Pooh is yellow with red shirt. Eeyore is two-tone gray with pink trim. Piglet is pink with a red shirt. Tigger is orange and black with a pale yellow face and belly. Mint condition: $10 set.

Disney Parks and Stores, circa 1990 to 1991. Hard plastic jointed figures 6in (15cm) to 7in (18cm) tall including, Pooh with name on shirt; Tigger, yellow and black; Pooh, no name on shirt and muted coloration; and Tigger, orange and black with tan face and belly. Mint condition: $5-8 each.

Merry Christmas with Pooh

Sears, circa 1970s. Painted, composition 8in (20cm) musical tree that plays "Jingle Bells" as it revolves. Characters include Piglet, Tigger, Owl, Pooh, Kanga, Eeyore, and Rabbit, all tucked into the tree. Ceramic 6in (15cm) Santa Pooh with blue honey pot as candle holder. Near mint condition, Tree: $75-100. Mint condition, Santa Pooh: $35-50.

Sears, circa 1970s. Glass ball ornaments featuring Pooh holding honey jar, in original box. Very good condition in box: $25-35.

Sears, circa 1970s. Pooh light set with ten gold flocked vinyl Poohs wearing red vests. Mint in box: $50-65.

Sears, circa 1970s. Set of eight acrylic ornaments including yellow Rabbit; gray Eeyore; tan and white Owl; orange, black and white Tigger; gold Pooh with and without red hat; brown Kanga and Roo; and pink Piglet. Excellent condition: $10 each.

Sears, circa 1970s. Set of flocked vinyl ornaments including five different Poohs, Tigger, Rabbit, Owl and Eeyore. Poohs include: Pooh with honey pot, stocking, candy cane, balloon, and clutching Pooh. Excellent condition: $5-8 each.

Top and Bottom:
Hallmark, circa 1979.
Satin ball ornament
from Hallmark featur-
ing Pooh and Piglet
with honey pots, Rab-
bit holding Tigger's
tail, and Roo riding
Eeyore. Mint in box:
$30-35.

Sears, circa 1988. Giant 48in (122cm) plush Santa Pooh
used as store display and sometimes seen without Santa
outfit. Pooh is a yellow plush with red sweater under a
red/white Santa jacket with red hat and black belt. Mint
condition, plush: $200-300.

Sears, circa 1988. Giant plastic Pooh to light up a snowy yard. Mint condition, plastic: $75-125.

Willitts, circa 1988 to 1990. Christmas plates and bells each dated for the years 1988, 1989 and 1990. Production ended with the 1990 series. The bells have a gold figural Pooh handle. Boxes feature classic Pooh illustrations. Mint in box: $30-45 each.

Sears and The Disney Store, circa 1988 to 1990. Left: plush 16in (41cm) Santa Pooh, gold with red sweater and red/white Santa jacket and hat. Made in Korea for Sears. Right: 10in (25cm) Santa Pooh by Canasa Trading Corporation sold through The Disney Store. Pooh is wearing a red sweater, scarf and hat. Mint condition: $25-35 each.

Willitts, circa 1989-1990. Above: 4in (10cm) to 5in (13cm) bisque musical of Pooh and Piglet carrying a tree in the snow. Entitled "Sing Ho for the Life of a Pooh" plays "We Wish You a Merry Christmas." 5in (13cm) to 6in (15cm) musical snowglobe of Pooh holding a candle. Plays "Winter Wonderland." Right: Christmas mug with Pooh and Piglet, entitled "3 Cheers for Pooh!" Mint in box, musical bisque and snowglobe: $35-50 each. Mint in box, mug: $20-30.

Circa 1988 to 1990. Set of six metal coasters with storage tin. Pictures Pooh with Piglet sitting by fire, entitled "Christmas is so much friendlier with two." Mint condition: $15-25 set.

The Disney Store, circa 1989. Flat, wooden ornament of Pooh holding onto big red ornament. Mint condition: $10-15.

Willitts, circa 1989 to 1990. Bisque ornaments: "Baby's First Christmas" with Pooh on a log looking up at honey pot, Pooh holding candle, and Pooh carrying tree. Mint in box: $10-20 each.

Bisque ornaments: Pooh holding blue balloon and Pooh holding present. Also available but not pictured are: Pooh writing letter, Pooh with picnic basket, Pooh in bath, and Pooh and Piglet on log. (Many of these are identical to the figurines in the chapter on ceramics.) Mint in box: $10-20 each.

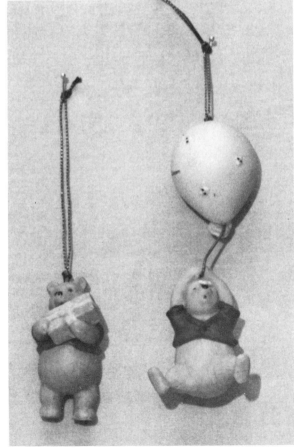

111

Left: The Disney Store, circa 1989 to 1991. Plush Pooh stocking with gold Pooh head and hands and red/white hat and stocking. Mint condition: $20-25.

Below: The Disney Store, circa 1990 to 1991. Set of 2½in (4cm) bone china ornaments of Tigger, Pooh, Piglet, Rabbit, and Eeyore. Kanga was also available at some stores but not pictured. Each figurine is decked with holly, scarf, or bow. Mint in package: $5-8 each.

112

The Disney Store, circa 1990 to 1991. Set of four 2½in (4cm) ceramic ornaments of Tigger, Eeyore, Pooh, and Piglet. Mint in package: $5-8 each.

Grolier, circa 1990 to present. Three ornaments available when subscribing to the entire set of Disney character ornaments. Left is Pooh 2in (5cm) playing a drum, from the regular ornament collection. Center and right are from the angel collection. Pooh angel 3in (8cm) is eating honey while Tigger angel 5in (13cm) is holding a bag of presents. Mint in box: $25-35 each.

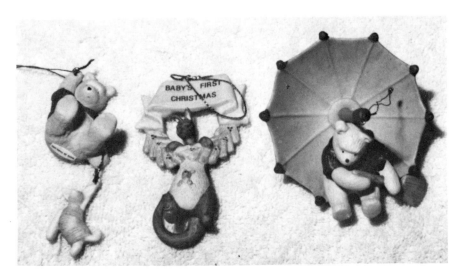

Willitts, circa 1990. Bisque ornaments of (Above) Pooh and Piglet, Kanga ("Baby's First Christmas"), Pooh in umbrella, (Left) Tigger ("Our First Christmas"), and Eeyore in stocking ("Baby's First Christmas"). Mint in box: $10-15 each.

The Disney Store, circa 1990. Papier mâché ball ornament with all the Pooh characters next to "Trespassers Will" sign. Mint in package: $5-8.

Danforth Pewters, circa 1990 to 1991. Set of four pewter ornaments including: Pooh eating honey, Christopher Robin nailing Eeyore's tail while Pooh watches, Piglet, and Pooh holding candle. Style is classic Pooh and each comes on card printed with appropriate background. MOC (Mint On Card): $15-20.

The Disney Store, circa 1990 to 1991. Flat, wooden ornaments, 5in (13cm) in height, of Tigger, Rabbit, Pooh, Eeyore, Kanga and Roo, and Piglet. There was also a 6in (15cm) Pooh ornament with moving arms and legs when string is pulled. Mint in package: $5-8 each.

Hallmark, circa 1991. Set of six ornaments ranging from 3in (8cm) to 5in (13cm), including Pooh with honey pot, Kanga and Roo with string of beads, Christopher Robin carrying tree, Rabbit holding red star, Piglet riding Eeyore, and Tigger bouncing. Mint in box: $20-40 each.

The Disney Store, circa 1991. Musical snowglobe featuring Pooh, Tigger, Eeyore and Piglet decorating a tree. Plays "We Wish You a Merry Christmas." Mint condition: $45.

The Disney Store, circa 1991. Left: Papier mâché ball with purple and white background. Tigger is carrying tree, Kanga and Roo are playing by a wagon of toys while Eeyore watches, Pooh and Piglet are looking at each other. Below: Flat, wooden, 5in (13cm) ornament of Pooh, Piglet, Tigger, and Rabbit with honey pots. Mint in package: $5-10 each.

Other Teddy Bear Books...

4th Teddy Bear & friends® Price Guide
by Linda Mullins. Latest "bible of teddy bear and animal values." This book shows and values what is being collected today. Teddy bears, rabbits, cats and dogs as well as a bevy of other animals. Features Muffy, antique to collectible, manufacturers and artists. Special sections on the ever popular Steiff, North American Bear, and Gund. 358 stunning photographs, 118 in full color. 6" x 9". PB. Item #H4438. (087588-399-0). **$12.95**

Contemporary Teddy Bear Price Guide
Artists to Manufacturers
by Terry & Doris Michaud. For the first time ever a book has been devoted to contemporary teddy bears. Contains select artists with current values for their bears and information on the artist. First scientific approach to pricing as a computer program was devised to estimate the current value of each bear. In addition to the artist bears, there is a section devoted to Steiff, Hermann and other sought after bears of the last decade. 179 color and 394 b/w photographs. 160 pages. 8½" x 11". PB. Item #H4437. (0-87588-398-2). **$16.95**

...Available from Hobby House Press
1 Corporate Drive
Grantsville, MD 21536
or from your favorite bookstore or Teddy Bear merchant.

1-800-554-1447

Call or write for a free catalog of the
world's largest selection of
books on teddy bears and dolls.

Carol J. Smith

Carol lives in Washington State with her husband and two young boys. She has a doctorate degree in Zoology and works as a Fish Biologist for the Washington Department of Fish and Wildlife. Her interest in Pooh items began as a child, when *The World of Pooh* was given to her by her parents, and has continued when extra time has allowed. She is most grateful for the wonderful friends she has met while pursuing this hobby. Other interests include water sports, gardening, and raising dalmatians.